# LOVE DAT CAT!

## 165 Ways to Make Your Cat Purr-Fectly Happy

by

# Jill Kramer

Illustrated by

## Mark Kingsley Brown

**CCC PUBLICATIONS**

Published by:
CCC Publications
1111 Rancho Conejo Blvd.
Suites 411 & 412
Newbury Park, CA 91320

Manufactured in the United States of America

Cover © 1996 CCC Publications

Interior illustrations © 1996 CCC Publications

Cover designed by Christy Allison

Interior art by Mark Kingsley Brown

Cover/Interior production by Oasis Graphics

(Some of the material in this book was adapted from Jill Kramer's book, Cat Love, published by Hay House, 1994. Used by permission of the author and publisher.)

ISBN: 1-57644-006-0

If your local U.S. bookstore is out of stock, copies of this book may be obtained by mailing check or money order for $6.95 per book (plus $2.50 to cover postage and handling) to: CCC Publications; 1111 Rancho Conejo Blvd.; Suites 411 & 412; Newbury Park, CA 91320.

Pre-publication Edition – 6/96

...And on the ninth day, God did sayeth:
"I shall summon My most beloved angels, and shall incarnate them as feline creatures, that they might provide loving companionship for humankind on this Earth."


Cat Proverb
Kramer 19:96

Dedicated to all of the catlovers in the world who have opened their homes and their hearts to very special angels heavenly feline beings who have incarnated as cats to provide loving companionship to us mortals.

## PREFACE

Do you adore your cat, as I do? Do you treat your furry little being like a member of the family, just as you would a parent, sibling, or child? Would you do just about anything to make your cat as happy as can be? If so, then this book is very much for YOU!

My cats, Sage and Dolly, are my best friends, my children, my buddies, my pals, my comforters when I'm blue, my cuddlers when I'm in need of love. They have feelings, personalities, thought processes, and frustrations...and don't let anyone tell you that "they're just animals." They're God's creatures, and they deserve the same attention and respect that human beings do. (Are you with me so far?)

I've written this book to provide you with practical (and sometimes humorous) advice for making your cat purr-fectly happy. I hope the information provided allows you and your beloved feline to enjoy many years of love, fun, and companionship.

Let's bring our cats into the next century with us so that they, too, can be a part of the wonderful earth changes that will affect us all.

### THESE ARE THE YEARS OF THE ME-ow GENERATION. LET'S MAKE THE MOST OF THEM!

Jill Kramer
Southern CAT-ifornia

---

(P.S. I am aware that many of you have more than one cat, as I do, but I have used the singular word cat throughout most of the book for ease of usage. Also, I have referred to cats as both "him" and "her," respectively, so that both Toms and Thomasinas will be represented equally.)

## ♥ CatHappy Tip #1 ♥

Get your little angel a kitty companion. She'll love the company when you're at work or out of town, and the difference between feeding one cat and two will barely make a dent in your budget...But don't despair if they fight like cats and dogs for the first few weeks. This type of transition is to be expected.

# ♥ CatHappy Tip #2 ♥

If you're reading this book but don't have a cat yet, please think about adopting one. I've often heard busy professionals say, "Well, it wouldn't be fair for me to get a cat; I only have a one-bedroom apartment, and I work all day." Well, my reply to that is: What's better a cat living in a 3x5-foot cage in an animal shelter waiting to be put to sleep, or a happy cat who lives in a nice, warm apartment with plenty of food and water and...an owner who does come home at some point? Think about it.

# ♥ CatHappy Tip #3 ♥

When introducing a new cat into your home, put a dab of the same perfume on each cat's head, so they will "recognize" each other's scent. It will help them get accustomed to each other much faster...and make your life much more plea-scent, as well!

## ♥ CatHappy Tip #4 ♥

I'm sure you've seen a little crusty material in your cat's eyes at times. Don't despair just wipe his eyes (in the direction of the nose) with some wet cotton or tissue. Now he can clearly see...how much you love him!

## ♥ CatHappy Tip #5 ♥

Avoid giving your cat any meat that may have bones in it, but you can give your cat treats from your table in moderation. Make sure you haven't overspiced the food, though. Kitty likes her food rather bland.

♥ **CatHappy Tip #6** ♥

Believe it or not, there are now "claw caps" that you can place over your cat's claws to protect your furniture...and eliminate the need for declawing. They last about 60 days, and you can order them from cat catalogs, cat stores, and your veterinarian.

# ♥ CatHappy Tip #7 ♥

Brush or comb your cat every day. You will not only remove the excess fur that can give him all those nasty furballs, but grooming also stimulates circulation and oil-gland secretions in the skin, resulting in a shiny and beautiful coat. (If you have more than one cat, and they tend to lick each other's fur, this is an additional reason to comb or brush your cats daily. If you don't, they'll accumulate double the amount of furballs!)

# ♥ CatHappy Tip #8 ♥

Get on your cat's level and have some fun! You know exactly what she likes to play with and it's probably a balled-up piece of newspaper as opposed to that $14.95 cat toy you bought last week. So, get down! She'll love you for it!

# ♥ CatHappy Tip #9 ♥

Give your cat bottled water instead of tap. It has been proven that cats can actually taste water, so the good stuff will really make a difference. And it won't be filled with chemicals and pollutants that can be harmful to kit-cat.

♥ **CatHappy Tip #10** ♥

Whether your cat eats dry food or wet or both, make sure you give him some variety. No self-respecting finicky cat wants to eat beef and liver dinner every single day! And, ilf your sweet little kit-cat's canned food has been in the refrigerator, let it warm to room temperature before serving. There's nothing worse than cold, congealed leftovers!

# ♥ CatHappy Tip #11 ♥

If your cat scratches a lot due to fleas, it's no fun for her, let me tell you (I know this because my cat told me so), so use a flea comb (the metal, not the plastic, kind) on a regular basis, and vacuum and/or shampoo your rugs often. Some garlic in your cat's diet can help combat those pesky fleas, too.

# ♥ CatHappy Tip #12 ♥

Let your cat sleep with you. You'll enjoy the warmth and companionship of a sweet, furry body next to you in bed, and sleeping together is a great way for you and your cat to bond. But don't squirm around too much at night 'cause ya don't want to wake kitty up, do ya?

# ♥ CatHappy Tip #13 ♥

You know how your cat seemingly disappears, and you search every nook and cranny in your home but you can't find her, and then after a few hours, there she is, and you can't figure out where her hiding place could have been? Well, the best thing you can do for your cat is to let her be. She needs her space, too!

# ♥ CatHappy Tip #14 ♥

The American dream is to own a home, correct? Well, your cat wants a home of his own, too. You can buy a nice three-level kitty condo at your local pet store. And just think no 30-year mortgage to deal with!

# ♥ CatHappy Tip #15 ♥

If your cat loves milk, but you find that it sometimes upsets her system, try giving her skim (or 1%) milk a few times a month. It won't taste much different from whole milk to her, and she will probably be able to digest it better.

# ♥ CatHappy Tip #16 ♥

If you have an indoor cat, make sure he gets some fresh air. If you don't have an enclosed patio or balcony, put a leash and harness on kitty, and take him outside for a few minutes every day. (Now, I must admit that my cat simply sank to the ground the first time I tried this, but maybe your cat will be more agreeable.)

# ♥ CatHappy Tip #17 ♥

And now...a few words about litter boxes. Have you ever gone a whole day without flushing? Of course not! So, please don't make your cat suffer! Scoop out or change the litter at least once a day. It makes scents, doesn't it?

# ♥ CatHappy Tip #18 ♥

You know that favorite sunny spot your cat likes to sleep in every afternoon? Make it a warm and comfortable napping place by laying down a soft blanket or pillow. You wouldn't want to sleep on a hard surface, would you?

## ♥ CatHappy Tip #19 ♥

And, speaking of resting places, you know how your cat always sits on the very section of the Sunday paper that you've just started to peruse? Well, let her. There are lots of other sections you can read instead!

## ♥ CatHappy Tip #20 ♥

If you're going to be away from home for much of the day, leave some tunes playing on the stereo so your cat can feel like he has some company...but no heavy metal, please...kitty can only take so much!

# ♥ CatHappy Tip #21 ♥

Before you bring home your new kitten or cat for the first time, do take her to a veterinarian immediately so she can be checked for feline leukemia, fleas, worms, and other maladies. If you have other pets at home, you wouldn't want your new baby to bring home any unwanted "gifts." And your healthy new cat will feel so much more comfortable!

## ♥ CatHappy Tip #22 ♥

When you go on a vacation, don't board your cat if you can help it. How would you like to sit in a cage for two weeks? For the same amount of money, you could probably pay a neighbor to take care of him.

## ♥ CatHappy Tip #23 ♥

Talk to your cat often. It doesn't matter whether it's baby talk or grown-up talk or off-key singing or gibberish. She loves the sound of her Mommy or Daddy's voice!

## ♥ CatHappy Tip #24 ♥

Don't ever forget who's running the show. It's your cat's home. He just lets you live there. So, make sure that if you're not going to be home for a while, you leave your heat on when it's cold, and your air conditioning on when a hot day is predicted. That's a good Mommy and Daddy!

# ♥ CatHappy Tip #25 ♥

If your cat sleeps in a basket, box, or even a favorite chair most of the time, make sure you clean the blanket, pillow, or cushion regularly. You wouldn't want to sleep on the same sheets all the time, would you?

# ♥ CatHappy Tip #26 ♥

If your cat has claws and spends most of its time indoors, get him a cat tree, a piece of cardboard, or a scratching post. If you don't, your upholstery will be his first choice!

## ♥ CatHappy Tip #27 ♥

Watch your feet when you walk around your home. Tripping over your cat will hurt him as much as it hurts you!

## ♥ CatHappy Tip #28 ♥

Have you ever been tempted to give your cat some of your dog's food? Well, please don't! Dog food doesn't have the protein that cats need, so stick to the nutrient-rich cat food you get at your local pet store.

# ♥ CatHappy Tip #29 ♥

Have you noticed that your cat loves nibbling on your plants? Well, you can keep him from doing this by planting some cat grass in a pot and letting him chew on that. Then you'll both be happy!

# ♥ CatHappy Tip #30 ♥

Always have an abundant supply of litter on hand. Not only will your cat appreciate it, but it may come in handy for you if there's a natural disaster and the plumbing stops functioning. It also works great on icy driveways.

# ♥ CatHappy Tip #31 ♥

Learn your cat's unspoken language, so you can communicate with her better. For example, when she yawns, she's not necessarily sleepy; she's telling you she feels peaceful and content. And, when she slowly blinks her eyes at you, she's telling you she LOVES you!

# ♥ CatHappy Tip #32 ♥

Did you know that cats hate aluminum foil? So, if there's some area of your home that you don't want kitcat to walk on, just put some foil down, and I guarantee you that he will keep his paws off of it!

# ♥ CatHappy Tip #33 ♥

If you or one of your housemates is allergic to cats, but a cat-lover nonetheless, consider adopting a Sphinx cat (a Canadian hairless). She will be so happy to be adopted by you, and so what if she's not a great beauty...it's what's inside that counts!

## ♥ CatHappy Tip #34 ♥

If you've been feeding your cat commercial cat food but would like to switch to the more nutritious stuff from the pet supply store, try mixing the new food in with the old gradually. If you start feeding him the new food exclusively, he will probably go on a hunger strike!

# ♥ CatHappy Tip #35 ♥

Give your cat a special treat today! If you think you're really going to enjoy that sliced turkey sandwich with your cat gazing up at you with those big eyes, think again. Take out a few pieces for him so you can both enjoy lunch!

# ♥ CatHappy Tip #36 ♥

When there are children in the vicinity of your cat, keep an eye on them. Pulling tails and otherwise terrorizing your puss may keep the kids in stitches...but kitty doesn't like it at all. Trust me on this!

♥ **CatHappy Tip #37** ♥

If you are about to bring home a new baby from the hospital, help your cat adjust to the new arrival by bringing home a worn article of baby clothing so your kitcat can get used to your baby's scent. Also, make sure you have Puss checked by a vet for any parasites, and update all inoculations, before your little one comes home.

# ♥ CatHappy Tip #38 ♥

Clean out your cat's food and water bowls every day. I've seen people refilling their cat's dry food bowls without washing them first, and I always think: Would you use the same food dish every day without scrubbing it first? Of course not! Remember: cats are people, too!

# ♥ CatHappy Tip #39 ♥

Catnip is fun, legal, and inexpensive, so give some to your cat from time to time. ( I like to sprinkle a teaspoon or so on my carpet so my cat can roll around in it in ecstasy.) I mean, it's not as if she can go out to the local pub every now and again for some cheer. You gotta help her out!

## ♥ CatHappy Tip #40 ♥

If your cat has persistent behavioral problems, it is a sure sign that he is unhappy. If you can't figure out the cause of the problem, take your cat to the vet or to a cat therapist (yes, they do exist). Kitty's happiness must be maintained at all costs!

## ♥ CatHappy Tip #41 ♥

Buy a sturdy and "cat-friendly" carrier for your cat. When you transport her to the vet and other destinations, it's no wonder she meows incessantly if you've packed her in a cardboard box without "windows"

# ♥ CatHappy Tip #42 ♥

If your cat is very ill, and your vet suggests that he be put to sleep, please get a second opinion! If a friend of mine had listened to the first vet she consulted, her 13-year-old baby would have been put to sleep several years ago. Fortunately, she went to another vet, the cat had surgery, and he is now a bouncing baby...17-year-old!

# ♥  CatHappy Tip #43  ♥

When your new cat mother is nursing her kittens, she requires more than three times her normal intake of food, so feed her as much as she wants! (And then make arrangements to have her spayed after that one litter!)

# ♥  CatHappy Tip #44  ♥

If your cat likes to sleep a lot, let her! You need your 8 hours, and your cat needs her...18 hours!

# ♥ CatHappy Tip #45 ♥

To ward off furballs, you may have heard that giving your cat a little butter (by putting a little on your finger) every day helps. Well, this is true. And, your cat will lick his chops with joy! (Petromalt works well, too!)

# ♥ CatHappy Tip #46 ♥

Think about taking your cat on vacation with you. There are actually motels and bed and breakfast inns throughout the country that cat-er to cats on the road. Ask your cat-friendly travel agent for details.

# ♥ CatHappy Tip #47 ♥

Does your cat have a problem with ear mites? To relieve his "ear"-itation, in addition to using the drops that you need to get from your vet, also dab the inside of his ear with a cotton swab to remove any visible mites. This will speed up your cat's recovery and make him feel so much better!.

♥ **CatHappy Tip #48** ♥

When you're watching your favorite show, and your cat is on top of the TV with his paw hanging over your favorite TV star's face, you might be tempted to move said cat's paw. But please don't. You'll make kitty mad. And anyway, you've got a great photo opportunity right before your eyes!

## ♥ CatHappy Tip #49 ♥

Now when it comes to drinking out of the toilet (your cat, not you), I vote no on this practice. You may think this will make a funny home video, but all sorts of bacteria are breeding in this area, so protect your cat from himself, and keep the lid closed   especially if you have blue water in the tank!

# ♥ CatHappy Tip #50 ♥

If you move your indoor/outdoor cat to a new home, keep her inside for at least a month so she can get used to the smell of her new residence. She uses scent to find her way back home when she is outside. (When cats rub their cheeks against objects in your home, they're "marking" their place, so to speak.)

## ♥ CatHappy Tip #51 ♥

If you do let your cat outside at any time, make sure he's wearing a collar and I.D. tag with your name, address, and current telephone number on it. If he got lost, you'd both be heartbroken!

## ♥ CatHappy Tip #52 ♥

You needn't bathe your indoor cat; she does a fine job of licking and grooming herself. The only exception is if she gets into something really dirty like that family of dust bunnies under your bed!

♥ **CatHappy Tip #53** ♥

The holidays can be a joyous time, but they can be lethal to kitty if you let her nibble on some of the flora of the season mistletoe, poinsettia plants,and holly berries are all beautiful but poisonous. And the water at the bottom of the Christmas tree or Hanukah bush is not good for lappin' up either!

# ♥ CatHappy Tip #54 ♥

Allowing your kitties to indulge in the little pleasures of life can be one of the nicest things you can do for them. And what they love best are those sweet, intimate moments like watching Mom file her nails or just cuddling up beside her. These sweeties personify the term simple abundance very politically correct these days, you know.

# ♥ CatHappy Tip #55 ♥

If you buy a new piece of fur-niture for your home, let your cat be the first to initiate it. After all, it wouldn't feel like a real part of your home if it didn't have a half-inch of cat hair on it, right?

# ♥ CatHappy Tip #56 ♥

Play games with string and balls and the like that will allow your cat to run and jump. If your cat sleeps all the time, maybe it's because she doesn't have anybody to play with. Boo hoo.

## ♥ CatHappy Tip #57 ♥

Spread the word about the joys of cat ownership. There are a lot of orphaned cats out there, and a lot of people don't even realize how much they'd enjoy adopting one (or more) cats until they try it. Your cat (who knows all) will silently thank you for your efforts!

# ♥ CatHappy Tip #58 ♥

The best way to give a cat a pill (so you both don't get totally stressed out) is to hold his head firmly with one hand while drawing it back so the mouth opens. Then, plant the pill on the back of the tongue and shut the mouth. Rub his throat gently to encourage him to swallow. Good luck!

# ♥ CatHappy Tip #59 ♥

Your cat loves to be stroked behind her ears, because this is one of those places she can't reach with her tongue. Your touch may remind her of her mother's caresses!

# ♥ CatHappy Tip #60 ♥

Learn to recognize the signs that your cat is sick. The first sign is usually loss of appetite, followed by runny eyes and a dull, matted coat. If she's coughing, sneezing, or vomiting, a trip to the vet is a must!

# ♥ CatHappy Tip #61 ♥

Does your cat like to drink out of the bathroom sink faucet like it's a water fountain? Do him a favor, and let him do so whenever he requests it. Cats don't have that much variety in their lives, so every diversion helps!

# ♥ CatHappy Tip #62 ♥

Really listen to the quality of your cat's different meows. If you're a cat owner in the know, you'll soon figure out which meow means "I'm hungry," "Give me love," "Play with me," or the ever-popular "Go away and let me sleep."

# ♥ CatHappy Tip #63 ♥

If your cat indulges in naughty behavior, don't ever hit her or scream at her at the top of your lungs that's so uncivilized! Instead, use a plant sprayer to thwart her actions. Believe me, she'll eventually get the message. Another thing you can do is put her in the bedroom with the door closed when she does something naughty. After the third time, she probably won't do whatever it is anymore, and you'll co-exist happily!

# ♥ CatHappy Tip #64 ♥

When you massage your cat, use your nails gently instead of just using your fingers; he'll feeeeellll good! And always run your hand all the way from his head down to his tail. That's how a cat knows he's being petted by a real catlover!

# ♥ CatHappy Tip #65 ♥

Before buying rug shampoos, disinfectants, pesticides, or other household products, check the warning labels. Some of these items are extremely toxic to pets.

# CatHappy Tip #66  ♥

If your cat seems a little lethargic at times, you might buy one of those videos featuring birds chirping and flying about. My cat sat in a chair for 15 minutes, transfixed by all the birdies on the screen. It was almost too cute!

# ♥  CatHappy Tip #67  ♥

If your cat is being particularly finicky and won't eat her regular food, don't force it on her. Cats have moods, too. Why not give her a special treat today!

♥ **CatHappy Tip #68** ♥

When you do your laundry, put a towel in the dryer that is specifically for kitty's use. Then, when you remove your clothes and they're all warm and toasty, you can put his special towel on top of the load so your baby won't get his fur all over that nice black sweater of yours. (But just in case, you'll always want to have a lint brush on hand.)

# ♥ CatHappy Tip #69 ♥

If you're wondering what type of cat to adopt, quiet, long-haired cats tend to adapt better to apartment life, while shorter-haired cats are better in wide open spaces. But, this is not a hard-and-fast rule, so just love a cat no matter how much hair she has, and you'll make her very happy!

# ♥ CatHappy Tip #70 ♥

If you must board your cat, really shop around until you find a place that's warm, spotless, and where he will get the attention he deserves.

# ♥ CatHappy Tip #71 ♥

If you have a party at your home, do your cat a favor and put him in one of his favorite rooms with food, water, and his litter box...then close the door. You can't assume that everyone who comes in contact with your beloved will bestow the respect he deserves upon him. Who knows how some inebriated cat-hater might treat him! (Naturally, a person such as this would not be a friend of yours merely an uninvited gate-crasher!)

# ♥ CatHappy Tip #72 ♥

My cat Sage loves sleeping near the window, but it's hard for her plump little body to fit on the windowsill, so I got her a cat window seat that attaches to the underside of the ledge. She loves it...I'm sure your baby will, too!

# ♥ CatHappy Tip #73 ♥

Before you cook a whole chicken, pull out the kidney, chop it up into little pieces, and give it to your cat. He will be in feline heaven!

# ♥ CatHappy Tip #74 ♥

Does your cat love lying between the pages of a good book, as mine does? Why not set aside a few books that are exclusively his to "get into"!

# ♥ CatHappy Tip #75 ♥

At any time of the year, but especially in the winter, keep the blinds or shades open so the sun can come in. Your cat loves to bask in the warmth of the sunshine! Also, he loves to watch the birds and make bird noises right back at 'em!

## ♥ CatHappy Tip #76 ♥

To calm your cat when she's nervous, sit her on your lap, cup her face with your hand, and gently rub your finger down the side of her nose.

## ♥ CatHappy Tip #77 ♥

Don't ever let anyone tell you that cats have no emotions. When you've been away for a long time, doesn't your cat act somewhat angry? Be particularly sensitive to his feelings maybe a treat and some extra lovin' will help bring him around.

# ♥ CatHappy Tip #78 ♥

Put some extra milk in your morning cereal so when you get to the bottom of the bowl, kitty can take up the slack. Slurp, slurp! But be careful of Cocoa Puffs, because any form of chocolate can be harmful to your kitty.

# ♥ CatHappy Tip #79 ♥

When you open a can of tuna, instead of draining the water or oil into the sink, pour it over your cat's dry or wet food. What a special treat for your kitcat!

# ♥ CatHappy Tip #80 ♥

If you live in a house and have an indoor/outdoor cat, you might want to install a cat flap to allow her some independence. But, be careful of neighborhood cats and other critters following kitty into "her" home!

# ♥ CatHappy Tip #81 ♥

When you're out of town, call home and talk to your answering machine for a while so your cat can hear the sound of her Mom or Dad's voice. It will make her feel less lonely.

# ♥ CatHappy Tip #82 ♥

If you use window fans in your home, be sure that they have some type of protective shield so that your cat's paws and tail do not get caught in the blades of the fan. That would be very uncool!

# ♥ CatHappy Tip #83 ♥

If your cat squirms a lot when he is at the vet's, talk softly or sing to him while he's being examined. You might also want to give him a little treat after he's gone through this "hair-raising" ordeal!

## ♥ CatHappy Tip #84 ♥

If you own a Dustbuster, try running it over your cat's body gently. Even though she may be frightened by the upright cleaner, most cats love to be cleaned with this smaller version of a vacuum cleaner. It's a good way to remove excess hair, and judging by the way my cat reacts, it must feel pretty good, too!

# ♥ CatHappy Tip #85 ♥

Cats' ears are very sensitive, so if you play a musical instrument, try not to play too loud...or at least take some lessons! My cats meow at the top of their lungs when I play my flute...so now I play in the bathroom with the door closed!

# ♥ CatHappy Tip #86 ♥

On very hot summer days, rub some ice over your cat's body. It can be very uncomfortable wearing a fur coat when it's 90 degrees outside!

# ♥  CatHappy Tip #87  ♥

Clip your cat's toenails every few weeks so she doesn't catch them on rugs or upholstered or wicker furniture. The best way to do this is to sit on a sofa with your cat under your arm and her hindquarters against the back of the couch.
Then push the claw cover back and clip the tip.
The perfect cat-icure!

# ♥ CatHappy Tip #88 ♥

Check your closets and drawers before closing them. Your cat has a sneaky way of disappearing into these areas when you're not looking, and you wouldn't want to leave home for an extended period with him trapped in a tight spot without food, water, or a litter box!

## ♥ CatHappy Tip #89 ♥

Keep a cat-care book in your home library for emergencies. There are many great books out there that give very useful cat-related medical advice (both preventive and otherwise), and if something happens to your cat and you can't reach your vet immediately, one of these books could be a lifesaver.

# ♥ CatHappy Tip #90 ♥

If your cat enjoys sitting in screened windows, be sure the screens are locked securely in place. I'll never forget the day my parents' cat fell two stories when the screen in their living room blew out on a stormy day. The woman in the apartment below saw a cat flying past her window! (Fortunately, Snowshoes the cat still had 8 lives left!)

# ♥ CatHappy Tip #91 ♥

Many cats are utterly fascinated by small children and enjoy playing with them (as long as the kids don't pull their tails, etc.). Maybe it's because toddlers are more "down to earth" and the cats like to be on the same level with their playmates. Whatever the reason, encourage this type of kinship it could turn into a lifelong love affair.

# ♥ CatHappy Tip #92 ♥

Cats generally detest leaving the comfort and familiarilty of their homes. So, when you or your friends are away, take care of their pets in their absence, and your friends will no doubt reciprocate.

# ♥ CatHappy Tip #93 ♥

When you're out lying by your pool, make sure you keep an eye on kitcat so she doesn't start lapping up the water. Chlorine is not conducive to good health!

# ♥ CatHappy Tip #94 ♥

If you decide to declaw your indoor cat's front paws (I'm not going to get into the controversy of whether this is inhumane or not that's for you to decide), make sure you use shredded newspaper instead of conventional litter for a few weeks after he comes home from the vet so his little paws won't get infected with litter particles.

♥ **CatHappy Tip #95** ♥

When your cat is sitting on your lap or when you're talking to her as she's resting on another surface, make eye contact with her as you speak. Cats appreciate this as much as humans do, and she will reward you by giving you purrs and contented blinks of the eye!

# ♥ CatHappy Tip #96 ♥

If you have more than one cat, let them run around your home and play with each other without interference. My cats chase each other back and forth across my apartment every night around 10:30 and then wrestle for a few minutes. I just let them be. Cats need to get out their aggressions just like humans, after all!

# ♥ CatHappy Tip #97 ♥

Do you ever have your home or apartment cleaned, or have repairs done, while you're at work? If so, make sure you remind all service people not to let your indoor cat out. Also, make sure that the people you let into your home like cats. You wouldn't want some sadistic person to play "Kick the Cat" with your baby!

# ♥ CatHappy Tip #98 ♥

If you live in an area where earthquakes, tornadoes, hurricanes, or other natural disasters occur, you might want to designate one person in your family as the cat caretaker the one who will be specifically responsible for seeing that your cat is taken care of in the event of one of these emergencies. Forgetting about kitty would be a cat-astrophe!

# ♥ CatHappy Tip #99 ♥

Stroke your cat under his chin frequently. The pleasure he derives from it is considerable. His look of gratitude will be worth every stroke!

# ♥ CatHappy Tip #100 ♥

A good way to cat-proof your home is to mount electrical cords on your wall with a Velcro-type fastening device so your cat will not be tempted to bite into cords that are lying on the ground. Such behavior can lead to serious burns to the mouth and face.

# ♥ CatHappy Tip #101 ♥

Give your cat a name as soon as you adopt her, and then call her by her name as often as possible. She will come to respond to it. But please don't give her an embarrassing moniker like Poopsie or Do-Do-Head. Cats need respect!

# ♥ CatHappy Tip #102 ♥

Why don't you buy your cat one of those cat toys that looks like a fishing pole with a feather on the end. I guarantee you it will become one of his favorites!

# ♥ CatHappy Tip #103 ♥

Leave your cat's whiskers exactly as they are. I once saw a guy start to cut his cat's whiskers because, as this misguided cat-owner explained: "They're getting so long!" I educated him to the fact that whiskers reflect a cat's girth and are their "feelers" in the dark. Hallelujah! Kitty's whiskers were saved!

# ♥ CatHappy Tip #104 ♥

Avoid picking your cat up by the scruff of the neck. This is something that cat mothers do with newborn kittens when they're body weight is minimal, but it is not appropriate or safe for humans to do with their grown cats. Think about how it would feel if someone picked you by the hair!

# ♥ CatHappy Tip #105 ♥

If your cat is severely overweight, please see a (good) vet. When I was a kid, I had a cat whose stomach touched the floor. Our vet (who obviously didn't know much), said, "Just feed her less." We finally took Samantha to a vet who specialized in cats, and it turned out she had a thyroid condition. After being given medication, she was trim and healthy in no time.

## ♥ CatHappy Tip #106 ♥

If you keep your cat's litter box in your bathroom, be sure to leave the door open when you're taking a bath or shower (depending on your living situation). When your cat has to go, he's gotta go now!

## ♥ CatHappy Tip #107 ♥

If you want your cat to use his scratching post (rather than your new sofa), try sprinkling some fresh catnip on it he might form an attachment to it very quickly!

# ♥ CatHappy Tip #108 ♥

If you don't know exactly when your cat's birthday is, make the day that you adopted her the day of celebration each year and then pamper, pamper, pamper (even more than you usually do)!

# ♥ CatHappy Tip #109 ♥

When you take your cat on trips, put the cat carrier on the seat next to you (where your cat can see you) instead of on the back seat or the floor. The trip will be less traumatic for both of you!

# ♥ CatHappy Tip #110 ♥

Read the labels on the cat foods you buy. Those which are filled with all kinds of by-products and fillers may not be nutritionally sound. Check with your veterinarian or a knowledgeable pet store employee if you have questions about what's best for your kitcat.

## ♥ CatHappy Tip #111 ♥

When you get home from the supermarket, leave the empty brown paper grocery bags on the floor for a while, so your cat can play. But don't forget to let the cat out of the bag before you dispose of it!

## ♥ CatHappy Tip #112 ♥

If you have a dog that tends to eat up all of your cat's food before he can get to it, think about feeding your cat on the kitchen table or some other surface that is too high for the dog to jump up on kitty needs his food!

# ♥ CatHappy Tip #113 ♥

If your cat has grime on him that only soap and water can remove, put him in the bathtub. Let him sit there and relax for a few minutes before you start "torturing" him with soap and lukewarm water. If you have sliding glass doors, he will be effectively trapped, so...good luck...and wear long sleeves to resist scratches!

# ♥ CatHappy Tip #114 ♥

Some humans love the smell of gasoline, raspberries, or fried onions. Your cat, however, would probably be in seventh heaven if...you left your sneakers or shoes lying around. She loves to sniff them and put her paws and head inside them especially after you've just taken them off!

# ♥ CatHappy Tip #115 ♥

On cold winter nights, lift up that comforter and let your cat sleep with you under the covers. It feels wonderful to have a warm, fuzzy body next to you, and your cat will love being that close to her beloved master or mistress.

# ♥ CatHappy Tip #116 ♥

If you have more than two cats, make sure you use two litter boxes instead of one. Even with the scoop-style litter, one litter box just won't cut it...because the box will fill up too soon and cause a big stinkeroo!

# ♥ CatHappy Tip #117 ♥

Does your indoor cat tend to jump on the balcony of your home or apartment, making you very, very nervous? You might want to consider screening it in so your cat can see out, but not get out! One of the worst weeks of my life was the time my cat Dolly jumped or fell off my second-floor balcony and was lost for seven whole days. After a week of sleepless nights, I finally found her...but now, the balcony is closed!

# ♥ CatHappy Tip #118 ♥

Designate a blanket for your cat's use and sprinkle some catnip on it so she becomes attached to it. Then, if for some reason, you would prefer that she sleep in another room, you can lay down "her" blanket, and she might be more amenable to the change in scenery.

# ♥ CatHappy Tip #119 ♥

If you want to keep your home a little cleaner and also make your cat's paws more comfortable, think about getting a litter catcher. You can place it in front of your cat's litter box and it will remove the litter from his paws after he's covered up his "work."

♥ **CatHappy Tip #120** ♥

Don't take your cat places that might scare her just because it seems like a cool thing to do. I once took my cat to the beach, thinking she'd enjoy a change of scenery, but she was so terrified by the waves and the sand that she shrieked at the top of her little lungs. She was not happy, to say the least!

# ♥ CatHappy Tip #121 ♥

If a glass object happens to break in your home, be sure to sweep up the glass and then vacuum, so particles don't get into your cat's paws. Another effective way to pick up small glass particles is to use wet paper towels. The glass adheres to the towels, and then you can dispose of the towels easily. At this point, you can use a Dustbuster to pick up any particles you may have missed.

# ♥ CatHappy Tip #122 ♥

If you're planning on traveling with your cat by air, be sure your cat is wearing an up-to-date I.D. tag, and try not to travel during very hot or cold weather, as the baggage compartment where your cat may be kept may not be heated or air-conditioned.

# ♥ CatHappy Tip #123 ♥

If your cat tends to look forlorn and even cry when you leave for work in the morning, you might consider putting down her food for the day right before you leave or getting her involved with one of her favorite toys so she doesn't notice you're leaving. Now if you're the one who looks forlorn and cries when you have to leave your cat, that's another problem altogether (although purr-fectly understandable)!

# ♥ CatHappy Tip #124 ♥

Before you let your vaccinated cat play with neighbor cats, talk to their owners to make sure they have had their feline distemper and leukemia shots, too. Vaccinations are not 100 percent effective, so even a cat who has had his shots can be infected by a sick friend.

# ♥ CatHappy Tip #125 ♥

A good way to warm up your cat's canned food in a hurry after it's been in the refrigerator overnight is to microwave it for about 10 seconds. Kitty doesn't like to wait the 30 minutes or so that it would normally take for her food to get to room temperature!

# ♥ CatHappy Tip #126 ♥

Check out your cat's teeth on a regular basis. Cats can get tartar buildup and plaque just like humans, but your cat (unless he has extra-special powers) won't be able to tell you if he has a toothache, so it's up to you to check him out every once in a while.

# ♥ CatHappy Tip #127 ♥

For the sake of your cat and all pets, you might think about buying a reference guide (through a cat magazine or your pet store) that reveals which manufacturers do and do not test their products on animals. Think about how you'd feel if your cat was being used in an experiment to test mascara!

# ♥ CatHappy Tip #128 ♥

The next time you bring home new shoes, remember to leave out the empty shoe boxes for a while so Kitty can jump in. If your cat is like mine, she'll wedge herself into the smallest box no matter how "substantial" (i.e., fat) she is!

# ♥ CatHappy Tip #129 ♥

Do you have a new kitten who loves to sleep in your hair at night? Well, that's okay   let her have her way. She'll grow out of it, and it doesn't bother you that much, does it?  After all, that's her way of feeling warm, safe, and secure.

# ♥ CatHappy Tip #130 ♥

Don't you just love it when your cat greets you at the door when you come home after a hard day's work? To make this a regular habit, give him a little treat when you walk in or just smother him with lots and lots of love. Chances are you'll see his sweet little whiskered face beaming up at you every day when you walk in!

## ♥ CatHappy Tip #131 ♥

If your indoor cat accidentally gets out and you can't find him, alert your neighbors to look for him, notify your local cat shelter, put an ad in the Lost and Found section of your newspaper, post notices with his name and photo, and walk around your neighborhood yelling his name! Losing your baby would just be cat-astrophic for both of you!

# ♥ CatHappy Tip #132 ♥

Avoid giving your cat the tuna that you buy for yourself (although the tuna juice is okay). He may become addicted to the strong taste and smell and refuse to eat anything else. Not only that, but tuna is not nutritionally complete and wouldn't be healthful to give your baby on a regular basis.

♥ **CatHappy Tip #133** ♥

If you have two or more cats, and one of them passes away, the other cat(s) might go through a grieving period that is similar to your own. Be extra attentive to your feline(s), and think about adopting a new cat in the near future to keep your cat(s) company.

## ♥ CatHappy Tip #134 ♥

Find a place to board your cat (or bring her to work if you can) when you get your home fumigated. Never, under any circumstances, leave her at home when spraying is being done!

## ♥ CatHappy Tip #135 ♥

If your cat happens to get paint or tar on his beautiful coat, the best thing you can use to remove it is petroleum jelly, followed by pet shampoo. If the paint or tar is profuse, you might have to cut away the affected area with a scissors.

# ♥ CatHappy Tip #136 ♥

If your little sweetie is sick, you might want to prepare a special "sick bed" for him. Put him in a blanket-filled bo in a quiet corner of his favorite room, and you might even think about putting a hot water bottle filled with lukewarm water in his get-well spot. He will appreciate your loving care!

# ♥ CatHappy Tip #137 ♥

Has your cat been sleeping with you for most of her life? And, for one reason or another, is her space on your bed now being taken up by a human? If this is the case, your cat may be rather miffed by this turn of events, to say the least. Think about making her a special bed of her own that is right beside your bed. It's the next best thing to bedding there!

♥ **CatHappy Tip #138** ♥

If you decide to hire a pet-sitter, make sure you get references, and then be certain that he or she agrees to clean the litter box, refill the food and water bowls, administer any necessary medications, and give your cat some love and attention for at least a half-hour per visit. (And don't forget to leave your vet's name and number, as well as a number where you can be reached in case of emergency.)

# ♥ CatHappy Tip #139 ♥

Do you meditate on a regular basis? I do, and I find that my cats tend to jump on my lap and purr while I'm in this relaxed state. Maybe this is a sign that cats enjoy the relaxed vibe that emanates from a happy, tranquil person try it sometime!

# ♥ CatHappy Tip #140 ♥

On extremely hot days, put your cat in the bathtub (sans water, that is) she'll love the feel of the cold porcelain on her fur!

# ♥ CatHappy Tip #141 ♥

To add some extra nutrition to your cat's diet, you might cook some fresh meat mixed with vegetables such as peas, carrots, or green beans; or mix some cooked egg with the meat.

# ♥ CatHappy Tip #142 ♥

When you are planning to move to a new home or apartment, keep your cat's needs in mind. Does the apartment have a lot of windows for kitty to sit in, and a balcony that will allow her to get some fresh air? Does the home have an enclosed yard that will allow her to play outside but not stray away from home? Think about it.

# ♥ CatHappy Tip #143 ♥

Do you and your cat live in a very sunny, hot climate? If so, and if you allow your cat to roam outside, some sunblock applied to his ears will prevent sunburn on this sensitive area. (Your cat will be especially prone to burning if she is light in color.)

# ♥ CatHappy Tip #144 ♥

I've mentioned getting your cat a kitty companion, but you might also think about getting her a canine companion. A puppy probably won't intimidate your cat, and will probably become her best buddy as they grow up together.

# ♥ CatHappy Tip #145 ♥

Does your cat torture your toilet paper roll, spearing it and clawing at it so it looks like swiss cheese? Why not just give her her own roll to play with on the ground   it will make both of you a lot happier!

# ♥ CatHappy Tip #146 ♥

Try not to have things around your home that will annoy your cat. If he jumps every time your door buzzer sounds or your phone rings, you might think about making some modifications to preclude such disruptions. (No, I'm not kitting!)

# ♥ CatHappy Tip #147 ♥

After you brush your cat, if you gently rub her down with a piece of velvet or silk or a chamois cloth, her coat will be healthy, shiny, and oh-so-pettable.

# ♥ CatHappy Tip #148 ♥

If there is a new (human) infant in your home, your cat may get understandably jealous of all the attention that the baby is getting. Make a point of giving your cat some extra TLC, and say his name a lot while you're doing it. He'll learn that there's enough love to go around for everyone!

# ♥ CatHappy Tip #149 ♥

If your cat is plagued by those nasty fleas, don't use flea collars, sprays, or powders they don't work! Spend the money to get a fleabusting company to treat your carpets and upholstery with a borax-like product or buy the product and do it yourself. Your fleas will be a thing of the past in a matter of weeks. At the same time you're having your home treated, have your cat professionally shampooed. She'll feel so much better!

# ♥ CatHappy Tip #150 ♥

Regarding food and water, keep the area where your cat eats as clean as possible (especially during the summer months), checking for ants or other critters that might crawl into your cat's food and water bowls. On very hot days, you might drop an ice cube into the water bowl to cool kitty off when she seeks to quench her thirst.

♥ **CatHappy Tip #151** ♥

Before you move into a new apartment, make sure the owner allows cats. If you sneak them in behind someone's back, you may very well be evicted, and your poor kitty will have to adapt to a whole new environment. He won't like that...and neither will you. Honesty is always the best policy from the start!

# ♥ CatHappy Tip #152 ♥

If your sweetie pie gets the runs, but has no other sign of illness, give him as much clean water as he wants, and avoid feeding him for a day or two. Then, when he's better, feed him very small portions of canned or dry cat food, or cooked meat (but no raw liver or milk, please!)

# ♥ CatHappy Tip #153 ♥

If you live in a snowy clime and you let your cat outdoors in the winter, be ready with a warm cloth to wrap kitty in (and, if possible, a cozy fire in the fireplace) when he comes back in.

# ♥ CatHappy Tip #154 ♥

Respect your cat's inalienable right to have his own space, indulge in his own moods, and engage in activities that make him happy. For example, if on one particular day, he chooses to curl up in the corner of a dark room for hours at a time, leave him be. He can be playful, frisky, and attentive to you on another day!

# ♥ CatHappy Tip #155 ♥

If you can afford it, you might think about trying out that pet psychic you saw on the community access channel. Wouldn't you like to know exactly what your cat's thinking? Well, maybe not...

# ♥ CatHappy Tip #156 ♥

If you are going to be away from home for a considerable length of time and will probably be home after dark, think about leaving a light on for your cat. It will soothe her while she's patiently (or impatiently) waiting for you to return.

# ♥ CatHappy Tip #157 ♥

Does your cat like to sit right next to (on top of) your computer while you work at home? If so, why not make it easy for her to do so. Clear a space on your desk so your baby doesn't have to lie on notebooks, pencil points, staplers, and other uncomfortable office supplies.

# ♥ CatHappy Tip #158 ♥

Stay calm don't get mad at kitty when she is regurgitating a big 'ol furball on your new rug. It's normal for cats (especially long-haired ones) to expel furballs every few weeks, and your baby really has no control over where she does it. (Hint: If you let the furball dry for a few hours, it's a lot easier to pick up and probably won't even leave a stain.)

# ♥ CatHappy Tip #159 ♥

When you do wonderful things for other people and cats, you are paying respect to your own cat, too, so...if you know any elderly or disabled (or just lonely) persons who could use some loving companionship, find out if they would like to adopt a cat. If so, you might want to help them do so and advise them on buying litter, a litter box, a food/water dish, and an initial supply of food to start them out. Cats can change people's lives, and vice versa!

# ♥ CatHappy Tip #160 ♥

Make sure you don't leave a glass with water or milk in it lying out on a table. My cat once put her whole head in a glass to try to get to some water that was at the bottom, and then she got stuck, and she couldn't get her head out! This could have been very dangerous if I hadn't been there to help her!

# ♥ CatHappy Tip #161 ♥

If your veterinarian doesn't automatically mail you a notice regarding annual examinations, use your own (or better yet, your mother-in-law's birthday) as the date when you take him in for shots. A healthy indoor cat can live up to 20 years these days!

# ♥ CatHappy Tip #162 ♥

Pick up this book periodically (and, of course, gift it to your cat-loving friends as gifts) so you will remember to do things to make your cat happy on a regular basis. It's easy to take the love, warmth, companionship, and loyalty that your cat gives you for granted. Doing special things for him will remind you that your cat is an extremely important and unique part of your life!

# ♥ CatHappy Tip #163 ♥

When choosing a kitten from a litter, cat shelter, or pet store, look for the cat that seems bright-eyed, outgoing, and willing to be held. He will no doubt make the best companion for you, and the happier you are, the happier your cat will be!

# ♥ CatHappy Tip #164 ♥

Never leave your cat unattended in your car with the windows closed! The temperature in your vehicle on a sunny day can get up to 10 to 20 degrees higher than the temperature outside, resulting in severe dehydration and even death to your cat!

# ♥ CatHappy Tip #165 ♥

And, finally, scratch her fuzzy neck, kiss the top of her little head, rub her arching back...Hug his warm, furry body; cuddle with him, shower him with love...do everything you can to make your cat(s) happy...THEY WILL ALWAYS BE YOUR BELOVED BABIES!

## About the Author

When Jill Kramer was 8 years old, a strange cat wandered into her backyard in Ambler, Pennsylvania. After it was determined that the cat's apathetic owners didn't want to keep "Puss," Jill's family adopted her, thus beginning the author's lifelong love affair with these furry angels. Puss begat Junior (a calico cutie who remained with the Kramer family), and Friskie and Cutie, who moved in with the family next door. (And then Puss was spayed!)

After the untimely car-related deaths of Puss and Junior on the mean streets of Ambler (a good case for keeping your cat indoors), Jill's family adopted Samantha and Selma Ann two of the sweetest cats east of the Mississippi, who lived long and happy lives. After moving to Southern California, Jill adopted Sage and Dolly, currently the feline loves of her life (and the inspiration for this work of cat literature).

And that's all you really need to know about the author...

(If you would like to contact Jill Kramer, please write to her in care of the publisher, or e-mail her at jkcats@aol.com)

# MORE WAYS I CAN MAKE MY CAT PURR-FECTLY HAPPY

_____

_____

_____

_____

_____

_____

_____

_____

_____

_____

_____

_____

_____

_____

# MORE WAYS I CAN MAKE MY CAT PURR-FECTLY HAPPY

_____

_____

_____

_____

_____

_____

_____

_____

_____

_____

_____

_____

_____

_____

# TITLES BY CCC PUBLICATIONS

**Retail $4.99**
"?" book
POSITIVELY PREGNANT
WHY MEN ARE CLUELESS
CAN SEX IMPROVE YOUR GOLF?
THE COMPLETE BOOGER BOOK
FLYING FUNNIES
MARITAL BLISS & OXYMORONS
THE VERY VERY SEXY ADULT DOT-TO-DOT BOOK
THE DEFINITIVE FART BOOK
THE COMPLETE WIMP'S GUIDE TO SEX
THE CAT OWNER'S SHAPE UP MANUAL
PMS CRAZED: TOUCH ME AND I'LL KILL YOU!
RETIRED: LET THE GAMES BEGIN
THE OFFICE FROM HELL
FOOD & SEX
FITNESS FANATICS
YOUNGER MEN ARE BETTER THAN RETIN-A
BUT OSSIFER, IT'S NOT MY FAULT

**Retail $4.95**
YOU KNOW  YOU'RE AN OLD FART WHEN...
1001 WAYS TO PROCRASTINATE
HORMONES FROM HELL II
SHARING THE ROAD WITH IDIOTS
THE GREATEST ANSWERING MACHINE
   MESSAGES OF ALL TIME
WHAT DO WE DO NOW?? (A Guide For New Parents)
HOW TO TALK YOU WAY OUT OF A TRAFFIC TICKET
THE BOTTOM HALF (How To Spot Incompetent
   Professionals)
LIFE'S MOST EMBARRASSING MOMENTS
HOW TO ENTERTAIN PEOPLE YOU HATE
YOUR GUIDE TO CORPORATE SURVIVAL

THE SUPERIOR PERSON'S GUIDE TO EVERYDAY
   IRRITATIONS
GIFTING RIGHT

**Retail $5.95**
LOVE DAT CAT
CRINKLED 'N' WRINKLED
SIGNS YOU'RE A GOLF ADDICT
SMART COMEBACKS FOR STUPID QUESTIONS
YIKES! IT'S ANOTHER BIRTHDAY
SEX IS A GAME
SEX AND YOUR STARS
SIGNS YOUR SEX LIFE IS DEAD
40 AND HOLDING YOUR OWN
50 AND HOLDING YOUR OWN
MALE BASHING: WOMEN'S FAVORITE PASTIME
THINGS YOU CAN DO WITH A USELESS MAN
MORE THINGS YOU CAN DO WITH A USELESS MAN
THE WORLD'S GREATEST PUT-DOWN LINES
LITTLE INSTRUCTION BOOK OF THE RICH & FAMOUS
WELCOME TO YOUR MIDLIFE CRISIS
GETTING EVEN WITH THE ANSWERING MACHINE
ARE YOU A SPORTS NUT?
MEN ARE PIGS / WOMEN ARE BITCHES
ARE WE DYSFUNCTIONAL YET?
TECHNOLOGY BYTES!
50 WAYS TO HUSTLE YOUR FRIENDS ($5.99)
HORMONES FROM HELL
HUSBANDS FROM HELL
KILLER BRAS & Other Hazards Of The 50's
IT'S BETTER TO BE OVER THE HILL THAN UNDER IT
HOW TO REALLY PARTY!!!
WORK SUCKS!

THE PEOPLE WATCHER'S FIELD GUIDE
THE UNOFFICIAL WOMEN'S DIVORCE GUIDE
THE ABSOLUTE LAST CHANCE DIET BOOK
FOR MEN ONLY (How To Survive Marriage)
THE UGLY TRUTH ABOUT MEN
NEVER A DULL CARD
RED HOT MONOGAMY
   (In Just 60 Seconds A Day) ($6.95)
HOW TO SURVIVE A JEWISH MOTHER ($6.95)
WHY MEN DON'T HAVE A CLUE ($7.99)
LADIES, START YOUR ENGINES! ($7.99)

**Retail $3.95**
NO HANG-UPS
NO HANG-UPS II
NO HANG-UPS III
HOW TO SUCCEED IN SINGLES BARS
HOW TO GET EVEN WITH YOUR EXES
TOTALLY OUTRAGEOUS BUMPER-SNICKERS
($2.95)

**NO HANG-UPS – CASSETTES  Retail $4.98**

| Vol. I: | GENERAL MESSAGES (Female) |
| Vol. I: | GENERAL MESSAGES (Male) |
| Vol. II: | BUSINESS MESSAGES (Female) |
| Vol. II: | BUSINESS MESSAGES (Male) |
| Vol. III: | 'R' RATED MESSAGES (Female) |
| Vol. III: | 'R' RATED MESSAGES (Male) |
| Vol. IV: | SOUND EFFECTS ONLY |
| Vol. V: | CELEBRI-TEASE |